Sociology Revision Book 2
AS-Level
Wealth, Poverty & Welfare,
Education &
Research Methods

SOCIOLOGYTWYNHAM.COM

ACKNOWLEDGEMENT

Special thanks to pixabay.com for allowing the use of their image on the front cover.

CONTENTS

Acknowledgments i

1 Wealth, Poverty & Welfare Pg 1

2 Education Pg 17

3 Research methods Pg 33

4 Glossary Pg 45

5 Index Pg 46

6 Your notes Pg 48

7 About the author Pg 50

PLEASE NOTE

First and foremost this is a revision guide book designed to supplement rather than replace your text book.
Test Yourself AS - Sociology books accompany this series and also are available from Amazon.

1 WEALTH, POVERTY & WELFARE

Social inequality

Social inequality refers to social disadvantage not inherent difference. The main social inequalities in society arise from social-class, gender, ethnicity and inequalities in wealth and income.

Wealth and Income

Wealth is the value of possessions owned by a person or group of people such as a family. For example the number of homes a person or family own.

Income is the amount of money an individual or group receives. Sources of income can be earned or unearned.

- earned income – salaries and wages received on a regular basis e.g. weekly, monthly or annually
- unearned income - interest earned from investments, savings, rental income from property

The ownership of wealth tends to be concentrated among a small number of individuals and families who tend to have a lot of assets and capital.

- asset - an asset is any item of economic value owned by an individual or business that which could be converted to cash for example a car. Assets such as personal property, shares, bank savings and property are known as marketable wealth because they can be sold.
- capital is the amount of wealth/cash available for use in making profits. A small number of people, hold large amounts of capital in the form of company shares or other investments such as pension funds, land and factories.

Two commonly held forms of wealth are property and capital. Property wealth - wealthy families can have large property portfolios consisting of properties held either in the country of origin or global property portfolios held across the globe. These can be subdivided into productive property and consumption property.

- **productive property** – is wealth which provides the owner with an unearned income such as homes or factory units which are rented out. Company shares which provide a regular dividend are also known as productive property.
- **consumption property** – is wealth which the owner uses or consumes and therefore does not provide an income such as cars, the family home, yachts etc.

Distribution of wealth - each year the government produces statistics on the distribution of wealth in the UK. Distribution of wealth describes how the wealth is shared across the UK.

Figure 1 below, comes from a report by the Office for National Statistics (ONS), illustrates how the wealth held by the top 10% of households is over 4 times greater than the wealth of the bottom half of all households combined and, over 850 times greater than that of the least wealthy 10% of households.

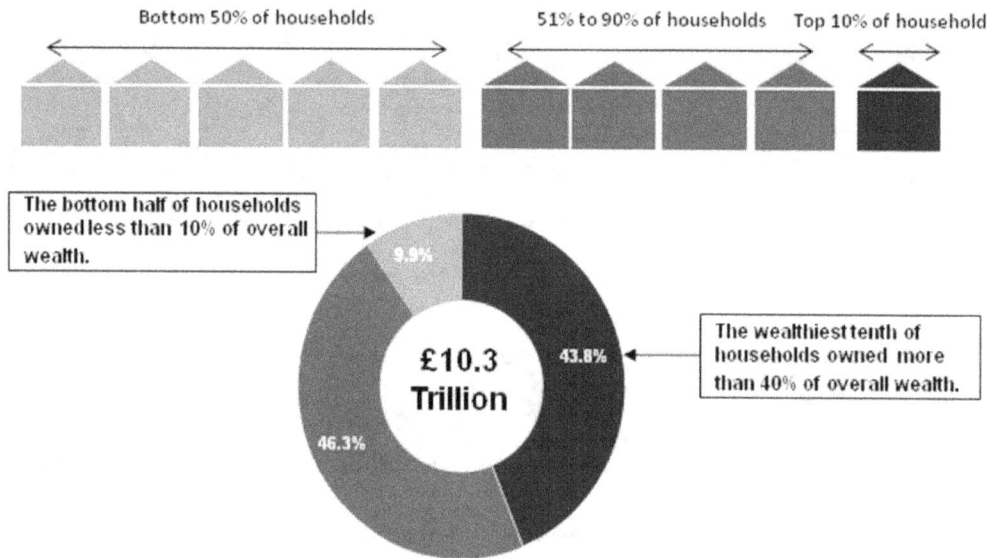

Fig1:Distribution of wealth in the UK 2008/10 Source: Office for National Statistics 03 December 2012

The ONS report also found belonging to the wealthiest 10% of household's required total wealth greater than £967,000. To be in the bottom 10% of the distribution, a household's value of total wealth needed to be less than £13,000 as shown in Figure 2 overleaf.

Figure 2 illustrates how even though homeownership in the UK has increased significantly it is evident from the above data the ownership of wealth remains concentrated in the hands of a small number of individuals and families.

Wealth Band	Total Wealth (£)
Bottom 10%	13,000
Bottom 50%	232,000
Top 10%	967,000
Top 1%	2,807,000

Fig2: Household Total Wealth Thresholds, GB, 2008/10 Source - Wealth and Assets Survey, ONS, December 2012

For most people the amount of money they have at their disposal comes from their income, this is known as disposable income - is the amount of money a household has to spend and save after paying their taxes. The amount of income a person generates is largely dependent on their job but it can also come from welfare benefits or interest from savings. Income that cannot be bought and sold, such as salaries and pensions is known as non-marketable wealth.

The amount of income a person generates varies widely. In 2014 the UK Treasury figures (figure 3, below) shows the top 10% of earners in Britain having salaries which are equal to more than the bottom 40% of earner salaries combined. The same Treasury data shows the top decile of single adults earning a median income of £60,500, compared to just £8,600 among the bottom decile (a decile is the separation of groups into ten equal sizes as depicted below).

Median gross income of households in decile	One adult (£)	One adult and one child (£)	Two adults (£)	Two adults and one child (£)	Two adults and two children (£)
Top decile	60,500	77,700	88,500	113,400	151,400
Ninth decile	39,800	49,300	58,300	74,700	91,100
Eighth decile	31,100	36,700	46,400	59,800	70,200
Seventh decile	24,800	30,900	37,900	49,200	59,900
Sixth decile	21,100	26,300	32,200	42,100	50,900
Fifth decile	17,600	24,700	27,200	35,600	44,200
Fourth decile	15,300	20,900	23,000	30,400	37,100
Third decile	13,200	17,000	19,900	26,400	32,000
Second decile	11,300	14,500	17,100	21,800	26,800
Bottom decile	8,600	10,700	13,300	15,300	19,700

Source: HM Treasury tax and benefit microsimulation model

Figure 3: Impact on households: distributional analysis to accompany Budget 2014 Source HM Treasury

It is evident from the data income distribution between social groups and the amount of disposable income a person or family has in the UK varies enormously. This is because many people have an income of less than 60% of the median income as illustrated in figure 4 overleaf.

- disposable income - is the money a person has left over after all taxes have been paid

- medium income – is the middle household income if all households in the UK were sorted in a list from poorest to richest (see figure 4)
- average income – in 2014 the UK's average income was £26,500

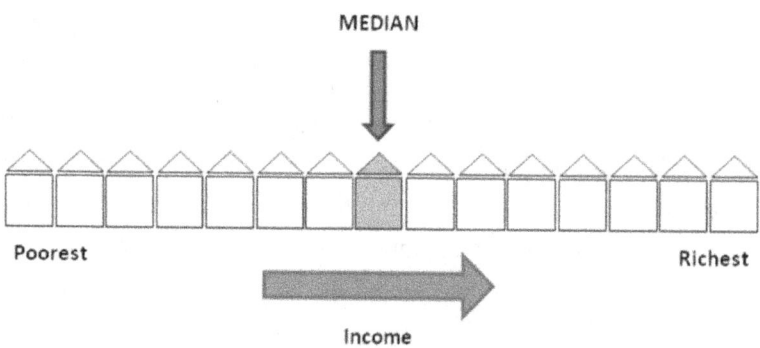

Figure 4 - Source: Office for National Statistics, 2014

Poverty

Poverty is a contested concept, as there is little agreement on how it should be either defined or measured. Therefore there are two fundamental ways of defining and measuring poverty.

- absolute poverty – is the lack of the minimum requirements needed for human survival such as food, water, shelter and clothing
- relative poverty – is a definition of poverty which is constructed with regard to what is the generally accepted standard of living in a specific society at a specific time compared to others. For example you could be seen to be in poverty in the UK if you didn't have a cooker, fridge-freezer, telephone etc.

The concept of absolute poverty was developed in the 19th century by Seebohm Rowntree who used the concept of a 'basket of goods' to measure poverty. Rowntree's basket of goods approach was used until the midpoint of the 20th century by early social scientists to measure poverty.

Strengths of an absolute definition of poverty

- conceptually it is straightforward for people to understand when thinking about donating to famine appeals
- it is easy to use when making comparisons across a nations regions
- it is easy to use when comparing poverty with different countries
- absolute poverty is easier to measure, and therefore easier to research

Weaknesses of an absolute definition of poverty

- often criticised as being simplistic for it assumes there is a universal concept of what constitutes poverty

4

- it is difficult to objectively decide what basic subsistence needs are
- it assumes the poor can shop around and get the cheapest goods
- it assumes the cheapest goods are available to purchase in the first place
- it ignores social exclusion - people are social creatures who 'need' to socially integrate by buying 'inappropriate' things such as gifts
- minimum diets do not recognise different the calorific needs of people. For example a builder might need more calories than an office worker

While absolute poverty focuses on the lack of the minimum requirements for survival, relative poverty defines poverty in relation to others creating social exclusion - is the lack of resources leading to the inability to participate in the normal social activities. Therefore social exclusion focuses on the broader cultural and social dimensions of poverty in addition to having a low income.

Using the concept of relative poverty, poverty is not fixed. Instead an individual's experience of poverty differs across societies, time periods and between different groups and the concept of poverty is a social construction.

Townsend (1968) introduced the concept of relative poverty in order to address the weaknesses identified in the absolute definition of poverty listed above. In order to operationalise poverty Townsend created a 'deprivation index' (as indicators of what seen as 'normal' for an acceptable standard of living).

To summarize Townsend's argument he:

1. identifies examples of poverty apart from income as being homelessness; poverty in health-care; poverty in education; stress; low-self-esteem; poverty at work; poor health and social isolation
2. uses a deprivation index to measure relative deprivation to benchmark an acceptable standard of living
3. finds a close link between relative deprivation and low income

Strengths of Townsend's definition of relative poverty

- it challenges the notion of there being universal concept of what constitutes poverty
- it recognises you cannot objectively decide what basic subsistence needs are
- it recognises the poor cannot always shop around to get the cheapest goods
- it recognises the cheapest goods are not always available in the first place
- it recognises social exclusion – how people are social creatures who 'need' to socially integrate by buying 'appropriate' things such as gifts
- it recognises minimum diets do not recognise different the calorific needs of people. A builder might need more calories than an office worker

Criticisms of Townsend's deprivation index are:

1. it is said to be measuring inequality rather than poverty
2. Wedderburn (1981) said the choice of deprivation indicators was not objective; the index consisted of items which reflected Townsend's own tastes and values
3. Piachaud (1987) argues the deprivation index ignores individual choice as some people might not have the items on Townsend's list simply because they didn't want them

Mack and Lansley's (1983, 1990) study Breadline Britain attempts to create a consensual definition of poverty in order to overcome the criticisms of Townsend's deprivation index. Their consensual definition came from asking a representative sample of the public to judge what they saw as socially perceived necessities which are necessary to maintain a minimum standard of living in the UK.

Gordon et al (2000) conducted their Poverty and Social Exclusion (PSE) survey on behalf of the Joseph Rowntree Foundation based on the Mack and Lansley's principles. Gordon (2000) found 24% of the UK population were living in poverty using Mack and Lansley's principle of socially perceived necessities.

In 2015 Mack and Lansley published their second study of Breadline Britain and identified the following changes:

- in 2012, 3 out 10 people in UK fell below the minimum living standard - twice as many as did in 1983
- 1 in 10 households lived in an damp home – a 30 year high
- the number of people who had skipped on meals had doubled since 1983 – from 13% to 28%

Mack and Lansley (2015) conclude life for people living on low incomes in Britain today is:

- one of a constant struggle to get by
- endless worrying about how to pay the next bill
- young people with little hope for the future
- parents cutting back for themselves to help their children

In summary:

The strengths of relative poverty as a concept are:

- poverty moves from being just about income to wider issues of social exclusion
- it highlights how poverty is relative to the society an individual is living in
- it highlights how poverty is relative to the time-period an individual is living in
- the concept of poverty is a social construction

Weakness of relative poverty as a concept are:

- it does not measure poverty but social inequality (there will always be those who have less than others)
- it is highly subjective, as any deprivation index reflects the value judgments of either the 'experts' – such as Townsend, the public, or Mack and Lansley.

Who are the UK's poor and wealthy individuals?

Who are the poor?

The poverty line is a government agreed dividing line separating those who are and are not poor. The key UK government measures take 60% of median income as the poverty line (PSE, 2015). Those with less than 60% of median income are classified as poor. This 'poverty line' is the agreed international measure used throughout the European Union (PSE, 2015).

The UK has never had an official poverty line instead it has two semi-official poverty lines.

1. the number of poor comes from the number of people claiming income support (welfare)
2. having less 50% or less of disposable average income (the EU's definition of poverty)

With the poverty threshold in 2011/12 being £128 per week for a single adult and £357 per week for a couple with two children the Joseph Rowntree Foundation report Monitoring Poverty and Social Exclusion (2013) (the report identifies people as being in poverty if their household income is below 60 per cent of the median -mid-point - income for all UK households) found:

- 21% of the UK population was in poverty – 13.5 million people
- 31% of UK children were in families in poverty – 4 million children
- 18% of UK pensioners were in poverty – 2 million people

Some social groups are more vulnerable to being poor than others: within those individuals who are classified as poor there are some social groups identified by Gordon's (2000) Poverty and Social Exclusion (PSE) survey where poverty is disproportionately high:

- non-retired people who are not working because they are unemployed (77%)
- disabled/sick (61%);
- those on income support (70%);
- lone parents (62%);
- younger people are also more likely to be poor - 16- to 24-year-olds (34%); 25- to 34-year-olds (38%).
- local authority tenants (61 per cent) and housing association tenants (57%)
- divorced or separated people are more likely to be poor (46%)
- ethnicity - higher poverty rate for non-white ethnic groups especially among the Bangladeshi and Black ethnic groups

As poverty is measured by net household income, adjusted for size (bigger ones need more money to reach a given standard of living than smaller ones) and after housing costs have been deducted there are also higher proportions of poor people in certain types of households:

1. those with 3+ children (46%)
2. those with youngest child aged 0-4 (41%) or aged 5-11 (35%)
3. households with one adult (38%)

It is important to remember the composition of the poor is not static but fluid. In 2014 Gordon conducted more research into poverty on behalf of Townsend Centre for International Poverty Research at the University of Bristol and found

- the percentage of UK households which lacked "three or more of the basic necessities of life" has increased from 14% in 1983 (around 3 million), to 33 per cent (around 8.7 million) in 2012
- one in every six adults **in paid work** are now defined as "poor"
- child poverty is projected to rise from 2012/13 with an expected 600,000 more children living in poverty by 2015/16. This upward trend is predicted to continue with 4.7 million UK children projected to be living in poverty by 2020 (Child Poverty Action Group, 2015)
- In Britain, the gap in earnings between the richest and poorest in the working-age population has risen from 8 to 1 in 1985 to 12 to 1 in 2008 (Telegraph, 05 Dec 2011)

To conclude – whether academics or politicians use absolute or relative definitions of poverty, poverty tends to be concentrated among certain social groups:

1. the low paid
2. the unemployed
3. lone-parent families
4. certain ethnic groups
5. women more than men

Who are the wealthy in the UK?

There are three main groupings which help classify the means by which the rich acquire their wealth:

- traditional wealth – these are people tend to be major landowners who inherit their wealth such as those listed in the UK's Estates Gazette magazine. Until recently the Duke of Westminster topped the magazine's list. But in 2013 his £8bn of assets could only rank him fourth.
- business wealth – these are people who own large corporations such as Richard Branson's Virgin business providing him with around £3.5bn of assets in 2015
- entertainment wealth – these are people who have acquired their wealth through music or sports industries etc. such as David Beckham with assets of around £250m in 2013 and Sir Elton John with around £300m worth of assets in 2015.

Some important points to consider about wealth:

1. most wealthy people do not work as hard as those earning low-incomes. For example cleaners tend to work long unsociable hours when all the offices or trains are not in use. While David Beckham only 'works' during a 90-minute football match or during training
2. the above three classifications of wealth above shows us how society values (and so pays) certain people more than others. For example an actor 'pretending to be a nurse' will earn far more than an actual nurse
3. as Thomas Piketty, 2014, argues "wealth originating in the past automatically grows more rapidly, even without labour, than wealth stemming from work, which can be saved." In other words wealth is increasingly coming from unearned sources such as inheritance rather than working (Economist, May, 2014)

Redistribution of wealth and incomes – (sharing the wealth)

In order to address the inequalities in wealth identified above successive governments have introduced policies which attempt to redistribute wealth and incomes - redistribution of wealth is the transfer of wealth and income from one individual or group to another individual or group by means of a social mechanisms such as:

1. social welfare benefits – payments paid by the state to needy members of society
2. income tax – tax paid on earned or unearned income
3. inheritance tax – a tax paid when people give gifts of wealth
4. capital gains tax – a tax paid when gaining significantly from the sale of an asset

Despite government policies redistributing wealth has been largely unsuccessful because:

1. failure to claim welfare - people fail to claim welfare benefits which are due to them
2. tax evasion – is an illegal activity - people do not declare their income or wealth. This ranges from an electrician being paid in cash and 'pocketing' the money without declaring it, to the rich 'hiding' their wealth abroad
3. tax avoidance – is a legal activity – people, mainly the wealthy, employing accountants to find legal ways of avoiding paying tax and therefore redistribute their wealth
4. tax relief – where the amount of income tax a person pays is reduced. This occurs when people pay money into their pension or make charitable donations. The more a person pays in to these areas the greater their tax relief which is why the rich have the most to gain from tax relief
5. tax cuts – In 1971 the top rate of income tax on earned income was 75%. The top rate of income tax was cut to 40% in the 1988 budget by Mrs Thatcher. In 2010 the Labour government created a new 50% tax band in 2010 for anyone with income of more than £150,000, but the coalition cut it to 45% in April 2013.

Why do the inequalities in wealth and income arise in the first place?

Functionalists argue the role of inherited wealth is an expression of ascribed status which was largely offset by industrialization encouraging meritocratic principles of achieved status and the accompanying material rewards achieved status brings. However Davis and Moore argue differences in income are necessary for the division of labour – whereby the world of work is fragmented into a large number of specialized jobs. From this position social inequalities in society are fair and just, everyone is given and equal chance. This helps build a value consensus around the view some people work hard, succeed and acquire wealth while others choose to be feckless and idle hence some people being poor.

The weakness of the functionalist argument is it ignores the continuation of inherited wealth being passed on by parents. In addition they assume everyone is motivated by material rewards. Plenty of people, such as teachers, are motivated more by the satisfaction gained by helping others than a high income.

Weber argues (Weberian explanations) an individual's market situation determines their status and subsequently their wealth and income. To understand the concept of market situation, consider how much a cleaner might be able to sell their labour for, then compare that to a doctor. The doctor has more specialised skills for which he/she can demand a higher price for. The weakness of this argument also ignores the power of inherited wealth being greater than their market situation.

In contrast Marxists argue inequalities are an outcome of the ruling-class owning the means of production (the factories) who exploit their position when employing the working-class. Being in the minority and owning the means of production the ruling-class capitalize on the profits generated by their working-class employees. The ruling-classes exploit the working-classes by getting them to work as hard as possible for the lowest wage possible. The ruling-class then invest their profits in more plant and machinery to generate even more profits. The outcome of such a process is social class inequality between the ruling and working-classes.

The weakness of the Marxist explanation ignores the upper middle-classes as they don't own the means of production but earn incomes large enough to earn vast amounts of wealth like Elton John.

Feminists would identify patriarchy as being the cause of inequalities between genders. As men tend to be in position of authority within the home and workplace they inevitably control the decision making. As Jan Phal (1993) found women are economically disadvantaged within the home as men tend to control and manage a couple's income. While in the workplace women's careers are often cut short to raise children constraining their lifetime earning potential. The weakness of this argument is it ignores the ability of successful women who rise to the top as well as raising a family.

The welfare state

Welfare is the mechanism through which people's needs are met in the form of payments paid by the state to needy members of society. The basic welfare needs the state meets are:

1. housing
2. healthcare
3. Income

There are four main providers of welfare (often known as welfare pluralism – because there is more than one provider):

- state provision
- private provision
- voluntary provision
- informal provision

State provision – the Welfare State grew out of the 1942 Beveridge Report which set out the need for a state system of social insurance (known as national insurance) to eliminate the '5 giants' of

1. want (poverty)
2. idleness (unemployment)
3. squalor (poor housing)
4. disease (poor health)
5. ignorance (ignorance)

This state system of free welfare services paid for by taxation included the National Health Service (NHS); compulsory state education; social security benefits now known as welfare; social service. The assumptions and principles made when designing the original model for UK state welfare provision were:

- women would remain housewives and mothers (in other words they would not be going out to work)
- there would be full-employment
- the principle of universal welfare for all
- the principle of free health-care and education for all

Private welfare provision – otherwise known as the free-market or New Right approach comes from private profit-making businesses delivering welfare services in exchange for profit as with any type of business. For example individuals in the UK are free to purchase their health care provision, effectively paying for their own operations in private hospitals.

Voluntary welfare provision – is delivered by non-profit organizations such as charities. This is also known as the third sector. Though they employ salaried staff, the non-profit-making organizations are funded by donations from the public and grants. These organizations include Shelter, Help the Aged and the Child Poverty Action Group which are also pressure groups. As pressure groups they can put pressure on those in power in order to raise the awareness of the plight of the poor in order to improve welfare provision.

Informal welfare provision – is welfare delivered by family, friends and neighbours (though the term informal welfare is more often than not a euphemism for 'free' welfare provision by women – see page 13 & 16). A lot of welfare provision is still delivered this way to the extent Mack and Lansley (2015) note how in recent years the burden of welfare is moving increasingly from the state to individuals and households.

Competing theoretical arguments about welfare provision

There are four main sociological approaches as to how welfare should be provided. These theoretical arguments help shape social policy on welfare provision.

However within these four sociological approaches, there are broadly speaking, two main theoretical positions. Those who see welfare as the responsibility of the individual (New Right approach – argues for means tested benefits) and those that see it as the responsibility of the state (social democratic approach – argues for universal benefits). A third approach – known as the Third Way (Giddens, 1998) is a way of reconciling the New Right and social democratic approaches.

Social democrats such as Tawney (1931) argue the welfare state should adopt a 'strategy of equality' in order redistribute wealth from the rich to the poor reducing social marginalization – (social marginalization is where some groups are forced into the margins by their poverty, ill-health) – through progressive taxation. The social democratic approach seeks to reduce social inequalities by passing income from the rich to the poor, helping to cultivate better social integration. On this basis welfare benefits should be payable to all – universal benefits - regardless of means.

However Le Grand (1982) noted how the middle-classes benefitted more from the NHS and state education which meant Tawney's 'strategy of equality' had worked within each social class but had failed to redistribute between the various social classes.

New Right views flourished during the 1979 - 1997 Conservative administration. Their free-market approach called for a 'rolling-back' of state involvement in welfare provision. Instead the New Right argued for an expansion of the free-market in the delivery of welfare. By reducing the burden on the state, the government could hand over a greater proportion of the responsibility of welfare to individuals and their families. This would encourage families to purchase their own welfare provision as and when they needed it, an example being the purchasing of private health-care insurance. By not having to provide welfare, the state would be spending less on things like benefits and so governments could reduce taxation putting more money back into taxpayer's pockets. More importantly the welfare burden shifted to the individual encouraging self-reliance.

In 1997 New Labour's Third Way was an attempt to find a middle-ground between state and private welfare provision. Tony Blair used the principles of the 'Third-Way' to provide welfare through the concept of 'rights with responsibilities'. The idea of 'rights with responsibilities' was envisaged in a 'work-society' where the work-ethic was a shared norm and value. Therefore an individual's right-to-welfare was in exchange for an individual's responsibility to seek work. For example improved benefits through Working Families Tax Credits encouraged people, especially mothers, back to work without losing welfare payments. Other New Labour polices built on the Third Way philosophy were:

- National minimum wage
- Health and Education Action Zones (see page
- more childcare places for 4-year-olds so mothers could go back to work
- 'New Deals' to help the young, disabled, long-term unemployed and lone parents back into work

However for commentators like Stuart Hall (2003) Tony Blair's use of the Third Way was merely the New Labour dressing-up free market welfare polices in social democratic clothing. In other words New Labour was moving away from a social democratic principles of welfare towards free-market (neo-liberal) principles of welfare.

Since 2010 the Conservative Party has again sort to design its welfare policies yet again on a neo-liberal model (free-market New Right approach) of reducing the welfare burden on the state. The Welfare Reform Act of March 2012 was built on the principle that work must always be a more attractive option for individuals than claiming benefits.

Subsequently Iain Duncan-Smith's (2010/15) welfare policies are based on the principles of the New Right which is why there has been the introduction of:

- a £26,000 benefit cap; a housing benefit cap of £500 per week;
- the introduction of under-occupancy penalty in social housing more commonly known as the Bedroom Tax
- switching Child Benefit from a universal to a means-tested benefit in April 2013
- and the switch from Incapacity Benefit to Employment and Support Allowance in 2011.

Marxists argue as capitalism is about the exploitation of one social-class over another then social equality is impossible. For Marxists like Miliband, the state is an instrument of capitalism which is organized to defend the interests of the ruling-class. Therefore the only way social equality can be achieved is by the changing the economic system – (we have a capitalist economic system).

For Marxists the only purpose of the welfare system is as an instrument of the ruling-class, as welfare helps pacify the working-classes. This is because the welfare system provides education, preventing absolute poverty as well as providing effective and free health-care to the workers and so needs to be defended.

The problem is state welfare provision ends up legitimizing capitalism as state welfare provision helps reproduce an efficient and effective workforce making the whole process acceptable – making welfare an ideological state apparatus.

Feminists argue the very nature of welfare subjugates women. Land (1976) points out from the very inception of Beveridge's welfare model benefits from women's unpaid social and biological reproduction in the home, it is women who are seen to take responsibility for delivering welfare of family members. Feminists are against welfare policies which help to reinforce patriarchy.

Explanations of poverty – cultural, material and structural

Cultural explanations - focus the attitudes of the poor, rather than the economic circumstances of the poor. Subsequently cultural explanations focus on the welfare state (sometimes known as the nanny state) for creating a dependency culture).

Lewis' cultural of poverty thesis (1961) identified the poor as forming a distinctive subculture. The poor's values differ from mainstream society through their differing forms of primary socialization. The poor seek instant gratification and present-time orientation instead of adopting the mainstream middle-class values of future time orientation and deferred gratification.

New Right commentators such as Marsland (1989) adopt such an approach arguing generous welfare payments remove the will-to-work creating a dependency culture which:

- undermines the ability of individuals to be self-reliant
- undermines an individual's self-responsibility and capacity for self-improvement

The above occurs because welfare payments:

- are traditionally universal, instead they ought to be means-tested, targeting those really in need such as the sick and disabled
- are traditionally too generous, with some such as child-benefit being paid irrespective of the recipient's income

It is worth reminding ourselves since the Conservative's were elected in 2010 Ian Duncan Smith has addressed many of the points raised above by Marsland. For example in the introduction of a Benefit Cap in April 2013 and the means testing of child benefit are seen as restraining welfare dependency.

Another New Right commentator Charles Murray developed Lewis' subcultural idea by arguing the poor formed a unique underclass subculture though poor primary socialization. Murray argues the underclass are identifiable by their:

- fecklessness leading to recklessness and juvenile delinquency
- fiddling and 'sponging' off the welfare system
- failure and exclusion from school and education system in general
- family instability brought on by high rates of illegitimacy creating lone parenthood

Charles Murray's cure for these four F's are to:

- cut generous welfare payments to discourage lone parenthood
- encourage self-reliance through paid employment
- promote institution of marriage

Problems with cultural argument

- Dean and Taylor Goody's research found recipients of welfare were reluctant dependents (they wanted work)
- Marshall et al, found little evidence to support Murray's view that an underclass existed
- Devine along with Mack and Lansley (2015) argue the poor are not the architects of their situation, rather poverty is caused by structural issues, such as the decline in manufacturing industries, poor schooling and globalisation.

Material explanations - start with the economic situation which then influence the attitudes of the poor (whereas cultural explanations above argue it is the values of the underclass subculture which creates their poor economic situation). Therefore the emphasis is on the structural inequalities created by capitalism, such as the short-comings of the welfare state creating a cycle of deprivation for those trapped at the bottom, rather than endemic cultural differences.

The cycle of deprivation highlights the way in which poverty leads to further poverty. For example being in a low-paid job, equates to poor housing in a poor area. This in-turn means you are more likely to attend a poor performing school leading to low levels of achievement, which in turn leads to poor employment opportunities and subsequent low income and poverty for the next generation (this links to how Marxists such as Bowles and Ginitis see the education system as reproducing social class inequalities).

Examples of how you can get trapped in the cycle of deprivation are:

- dead-end jobs, are low-paid, meaning you are unable to save for future and 'escape' your circumstances
- zero hour contracts, provides an erratic income, leads to anxiety about paying the rent and so suffer mental health issues and so lose your job unemployment, leads to using loan-sharks or pay-day loans to buy necessities; loans charged at high interest rates which 'takes' more of your welfare leaving you with less money
- low income threating a stable family life due to increased arguments over money or working excessive hours simply to get-by

It is the above material processes which cultivate the attitudes and behaviours, such as instant gratification, of the poor rather them having an innate or 'inherited' culture of fecklessness and welfare dependency.

Structural explanations

Structural explanations focus on the unequal distribution of wealth, power an income arising from capitalism. Poverty is seen as an outcome of the inequalities inherent in capitalism rather than merely individual failings. Marxist, Weberian, Feminist and Functionalist are all structural explanations each with their own unique point of view:

Marxist explanations see the poor as an inevitable outcome of ruling-class exploitation and so inevitably remain poor. Miliband and Westergaard and Resler identify

- poverty as an outcome of capitalist exploitation keeping wages low helping to provide a pool of cheap labour
- poverty helps divide the working-class and so prevents the development of working-class unity that could overthrow capitalism
- poverty as well as the fear of becoming poor helps motivate the working-classes, which helps create an obedient workforce as well as an endless supply of cheap labour

Weber's explanation (known as Weberian approach) adopted by Townsend argues the different market position of individuals (the type of skills they have) creates the inequality

- poverty arises from having a weak position in the job market, unskilled and unqualified individuals a weak position in the job market as it is difficult to change their ranking in the job market
- illness, disability, unemployment all contribute to give individuals a weak position in the job market as it is difficult to change their ranking in the job market
- Weber argues the poor remain entrenched in poverty as they do not have the financial means to change their status

Feminist explanations would point to the number of women in poverty as illustrating the structural impact of patriarchal power on women's status in society. Glendinning and Millar (1992) argue there is a feminisation of poverty. While Oppenheimer and Harker (1996) research found more women than men are in poverty. Much of this feminisation of poverty is due to:

- most women are responsible for childcare, housework and other caring responsibilities such as for relatives while are all unpaid responsibilities
- women are more likely to be lone parents
- women are more likely to sacrifice their own standard of living for their children
- as women are more likely to take time away from their careers to raise children they tend to made fewer pension contributions or accept more flexible and lower paid employment on returning to work
- women live longer than men and so with possibly fewer pension contributions they might not be entitled to full-state pension or private pension and so are more dependent on state benefits for much longer

Functionalist explanations such as those by Davis and Moore see the poor as an integral part of a functioning society hence why the poor remain poor, they help maintain a functioning society by:

- poverty encourages the poor to do the dirty and dangerous jobs most people would want to do
- low pay helps keep service, clothing and catering industries
- the existence of poverty creates work in occupations like social work, the police etc
- the fear of failing into poverty motivates people to work which in turn establishes a collective consciousness around the value consensus of hard-work, honesty and planning for the future

2 EDUCATION

SCHOOL SYSTEM AND TYPES OF SCHOOLS

In the same way politicians sought to promote certain types of family structures, they have and continue to influence the types of school there are in England and Wales through their social policies.

1944 Education Act – established 3 types of schools known as the tripartite system – grammar; technical and secondary modern schools. A process of selection via 11+ test determined which school you went to. The top 15-20% of those passing the 11+ went to grammar schools

Criticisms of tripartite system:

- 11+ was unreliable;

- the selection process was unfair and wasteful;

- cemented social-class divisions

Comprehensive Schools – unlike the tripartite system there is no selection test for entry to comprehensive schools. The development of comprehensive schools came in the 1960s as a reaction against tripartite system (but process of selection still occurs in some areas of England).

Comprehensives sought to:

- reduce social class divisions;

- break down social-class barriers

Conservative education policy (1979 – 1997)

- New Vocationalism 1986 (NVQs etc);

- The 1988 Education Reform Act introduced competition between schools and turned parents into 'consumers' of education. This process is often termed the marketization (free market) of education.

New Right thinkers argue social policies are more effective if they are driven by free market principles. These principles are evident in the 1988 Education Act because the act introduced (in no particular order):

1. The National Curriculum
2. National testing (SATS)
3. National league tables
4. Open enrolment and parental choice
5. Ofsted
6. Local management of schools

New Labour's educational policy 1997 – 2010

- Specialist schools;
- Expansion of league tables (vocational GCSEs added as well as Contextual Value Added Scores);
- Equality of opportunity e.g. EMA; Education Action Zones (known as compensatory education)- page 23
- Expansion of numbers in FE and HE;
- Expansion of vocational education

Conservatives 2010 onwards

- Academies Bill;
- Free Schools:
- Bursary Scheme (replaced EMA);
- Vocational GCSEs axed from league tables;
- Changes to A-levels and GCSES
- Since 2010 there is now an even wider range of schools children can attend: Free schools, traditional Academies and Academy Converters all have the same status in law.

Independent Schools otherwise known as fee-paying schools are independent of government control.

COMPETING PERSPECTIVES OF EDUCATION

Functionalist perspective of education - Emile Durkheim – writing over 100 years ago, argued one of the main functions of education is to bind members of society together – this creates social unity and social solidarity. Therefore like the family, education is seen as a functional prerequisite because it helps pass on society's core values such as the division of labour.

Talcott Parsons writing in the 1950s developed Durkheim's ideas. He identified socialization (secondary) and social integration as two key functions of education, along with role allocation. Like Davis and Moore, Parsons' argued the education system functions to put the right people in the right jobs through a meritocratic system of role allocation.

For functionalists the key functions (purpose) of the education system are:

1. passes on society's culture – education helps establish a value consensus through the hidden curriculum (the hidden curriculum – how students learn behaviours, values, beliefs, and attitudes)
2. socialization - Parsons argues how schools take over the role of parents as sites of secondary socialization.
3. provides a bridge between particularistic values and universalistic values – schooling equips individuals with achieved status rather than ascribed status
4. provides a trained and qualified labour force – schooling equips people in society with the right skills needed to do their jobs creating a division of labour
5. meritocracy - Davis and Moore said the education system becomes the best mechanism for rewarding individual effort legitimising social inequalities

Marxist perspective of education - Louis Althusser (1971) argued that the main role of education in a capitalist society is the reproduction of an efficient and obedient work force. The working-class are 'accept' their exploitation by the ruling-class through several ideological state apparatuses such as the family and the education system. The education system is a particularly powerful ideological state apparatus because:

1. reinforces the ideology that capitalism is just and reasonable (schools teach pupils competition between each other is normal)

2. education system trains future workers to become submissive to authority (schools teaches pupils to accept being told what to do as normal, that way, when your boss orders you what to do, it seems perfectly normal)

Bowles and Gintis' study 'Schooling in Capitalist America' (1976) supported Althusser's ideas that there is a close correspondence (relationship) 'the correspondence principle' between the social relationships in the classroom and those in the workplace through:

1. the correspondence principle – schools processes are very similar to offices and factories, creating a long shadow of work through a system of top-down control and a hidden curriculum encouraging conformity

2. **myth of meritocracy** - schools legitimate the myth that everyone has an equal chance; so pupils think those people in the top jobs got there on merit when in fact those at the top are there due to their social-class background. In this way social inequality is legitimized and justified as natural

3. **hidden curriculum** – the school processes mentioned above which prepare students for workplace (rather than scholastic achievement) are reinforced through having to follow a timetable; being punctual; wearing a uniform; doing homework, are all part of the hidden curriculum (the 'visible' curriculum is your lessons, school assemblies, etc).

Bourdieu also sees the education system as reproducing and legitimizing social inequalities through his concept of social capital in order to explain how the middle-classes succeed while the working-class are less likely to (see page 22).

Paul Willis also adopts a Marxist approach when he studied the relationship between the education system and the workplace. His interactionist approach looked at working-class subcultural resistance (counter-culture) to the education system (see page 23).

Both functionalists and Marxists refer to the hidden curriculum. However they have distinct differences:

Functionalism and the hidden curriculum (positive)	Marxism and the hidden curriculum (negative)
1. pupils to look smart via the school uniform	1. school rules, detentions & rewards, teach people to conform whether you like it or not!
2. punctuality through disciplining people who are late	2. school assemblies teach respect for dominant ideas
3. shows children how to follow instructions	3. boys and girls to accept different roles in society with boys learning to be masculine and girls feminine
4. how to read and follow a timetable	4. to follow teachers' instructions without question in the same way you have to follow a bosses orders
5. teaches meritocracy - the benefits of working hard and doing additional work at home (homework)	5. being punctual, as your time belongs to your teacher/school and not you. This again replicates the way a future boss owns your time and so you're being prepared for the world of work!

Both functionalist and Marxist perspectives have other similarities:

- They are both structuralist approaches

- They both tend to ignore social processes within school (factors inside school) – except Willis

- They both tend to ignore the effect of the hidden curriculum on gender stereotyping

Despite their similarities functionalist and Marxist perspectives have their problems:

Problems with functionalism	Problems with Marxism
1. Differences in achievement in terms of gender, ethnicity and class questions the notion of a meritocratic education system 2. Education does not prepare students for the workplace as employers are often critical of the education system 3. It does not adequately explain how education serves the interests of certain groups through promoting certain values and ideologies	1. It assumes pupils are passive victims in the classroom – a point raised by Paul Willis 2. Most people see the inequalities in the education system and some parents challenge it by paying for their child's education 3. Some students work hard to overcome the inherent inequalities in the education system

Feminist perspective of education - for feminists the education system reinforces the social inequalities between the genders. This is achieved through:

1. gendered language – reflecting wider society, school textbooks (and teachers) tend to use gendered language – 'he', 'him', 'his' etc making women invisible
2. gendered roles – school textbooks have tended to present males and females in traditional gender roles – for example, women as mothers and housewives
3. gender stereotypes – reading schemes have also tended to present traditional gender stereotypes e.g 'boys are presented as more adventurous than girls'
4. women in the curriculum – in terms of what's taught in schools – the curriculum – women tend to be missing, in the background, or in second place and so 'hidden' from the curriculum mirroring society
5. subject choice – traditionally certain subjects were often seen as 'boys' subjects' and 'girls' subjects

Feminist perspectives have been valuable for exposing gender inequality in education. Partly as a result of sociological research, a lot has changed – for example, much of the sexism in reading schemes has now disappeared. Today, women have overtaken men on most measures of educational attainment.

FACTORS INSIDE SCHOOL AND FACTORS OUTSIDE SCHOOL AFFECTING ACHIEVEMENT

Despite numerous forms of social policy interventions by the state, significant class differences in educational achievement continue. Some sociologists focus on factors outside school as the primary cause for social class differences in educational achievement while others focus on factors inside school.

FACTORS OUTSIDE SCHOOL (material, cultural, linguistic deprivation and subcultural explanations)

Material deprivation

- Douglas' (1964) research identified material factors as the cause of working-class underachievement in schools. Material factors include, poor housing, poor diet etc. Gibson and Asthana (1999) found the greater the level of family disadvantage the smaller the percentage of students gaining 5 or more GCSE grades A* - C.

- A more recent piece of research by Lisa Harker (2006) also found a relationship between poor-quality housing and low attainment at school. Harker's research found:

1. less space to play, restricted a child's cognitive development
2. there was less space to study
3. increased likelihood of being bullied at school which increased truancy rates
4. higher stress levels of the parents, leading to less support

- Martha Farah (2006) researched the impact of socio-economic status on cognitive development and found that poverty had a direct impact on the development of a child's brain which ultimately affected their attainment at school.

- Furthermore the Sutton Trust (2005) found a direct relationship between free school meals and attainment. Top performing state schools had around 3% of their intake eligible for free school meals, whereas the majority of state schools had 14.5% of their intake eligible for free school meals.

Cultural deprivation

- Douglas also found cultural factors played an important part in a child's attainment at school. Douglas found middle-class parents compared to working-class parents:

1. took greater the parental interest in a child's education the greater the educational success
2. were better educated themselves and so better understood education system
3. more confident in dealing with schools/teachers
4. better able to help their child with school work

Cultural Capital

Bourdieu uses the term habitus to describe the cultural characteristics and values of each social-class. His point is middle-class children tend to thrive in school, as the culture of schooling is one which engages with cultural capital because:

1. cultural capital – the knowledge, language and values which readily translate into educational capital

2. upper and middle-class children succeed in school as they have more cultural capital

3. working-class children tend to lack cultural capital and so are more likely to fail in an educations system which 'enjoys' cultural capital

4. Bourdieu's point is that school looks like it Is culturally neutral when it is biased towards the upper and middle-classes

Subcultural explanations

- Cultural differences are extended further by examining sub-cultural differences between social groups. Sugarman (1970) and Hyman (1967) highlighted the effects of socialization:

    1. Middle-classes socialised their children to – focus on future time orientation and deferred gratification facilitated by individual effort
    2. Working-classes socialised their children to – focus on present time orientation and immediate gratification due to a sense of fatalism

Linguistic deprivation – language and education

- Educational success is heavily dependent on language. Bernstein (1971) distinguished between restricted speech codes (can be used by both social classes but mainly lower working classes) and elaborated speech codes (used by middle-classes).

Compensatory education (positive discrimination) is used by the state to compensate for the social inequalities identified above affecting educational outcomes. Examples are:

    1. Operation Head Start;
    2. Educational Action Zones;
    3. Educational Priority Areas;
    4. Pupil Premium; 16 – 19 Bursary Fund

Factors Inside School (interactionist perspective) school organization, teacher interaction and pupil subcultures

The interactionist perspective does not see pupils as passive 'victims'- of material or cultural forces but as active in their relationships with teachers and their schools e.g. school council influencing the meaning they give to a situation.

School organisation

- Keddie (1971) challenges the notion of cultural deprivation, discussed above, as the root cause of educational failure. Instead Keddie shines the spotlight on schools themselves as failing to meet the needs of cultural diversity.

- Rutter (1979) also places a greater emphasis on schools themselves. The better their organizational structures and polices the better the school; policies such as: (listed overleaf)

1. homework policy
2. marking policy
3. teacher reward systems
4. mixed ability classes
5. teacher lesson preparedness

Teacher interaction

- Becker's research found teachers had a stereotypical image of an ideal pupil based on middle-class qualities, labelling the ideal pupil as bright and successful, the halo-effect. In contrast teachers stereotyped working-class pupils as lacking motivation and difficult to manage therefore are negatively labelled as thick or slow.

- Rosenthal and Jacobson (1968) research found positive and negative labels helped produce a self-fulfilling prophecy in the classroom, highlighting the value of an interactionist approach as pupils clearly 'active' in their relationships with teachers.

- Ball's study of Beachside Comprehensive examined the effect of banding and streaming on pupil performance. Ball found top stream students were warmed up while lower streamed/banded pupils were cooled down. Streaming of banding is often linked to social class – the higher your social class the higher the likelihood of being in a top stream/band.

    1. setting is where pupils of similar ability are put in different groups/sets in specific subjects
    2. streaming/banding involves grouping students of similar ability for every subject studied.

PUPIL SUBCULTURES

Male anti-school subcultures

- Hargreaves (1967) related the emergence of pupil subcultures to labelling and streaming. Colin Lacey's (1970) study of Hightown Grammar school also showed how streaming can lead to the creation of anti-school subcultures. Paul Willis (1997) in 'Learning to Labour' examined the effects of being placed in lower bands/streams. Though Willis adopted a Marxist approach he drew much from the interactionist perspective to compensate for the failings of the traditional Marxist model. Willis found working-class pupils rebelled against their being labelled as failures by acting the fool in lessons in order to enhance their status/self-esteem in ways other than academic ones.

Mac an Ghaill (1994) identified 3 working-class male subcultures

1. Macho Lads;

2. Academic Achievers

3. New Enterprisers

Female subcultures

- Scott Davis (1995) found girls' resistance to school was evident but less aggressive than their male counterparts due to their preoccupation with 'romance' and any future domestic roles. Abrahams (1995) identified female resistance to school as one based on pushing school rules to the limit. While Osler and Vincent (2003) suggest that girls are more likely to develop patterns of non-attendance when facing difficulties in school

- Margret Fuller (1984) found African Caribbean girls formed positive subcultures by working extra hard, determined to succeed despite experiencing racism in schools. In contrast C. Jackson (2006) 'Lads and Ladettes in School: Gender and the Fear of Failure' looked at how girls are forming anti-school subcultures and becoming ladettes because of the fear of academic failure.

African-Caribbean male subcultures

- Gaine and George (1999) found African-Caribbean subcultures develop from both factors inside and outside school.

African-Caribbean female subcultures

- Mac an Ghail (1998) found in general African –Caribbean girls are pro-education and ambitious. Margret Fuller (1984) found African Caribbean girls formed positive subcultures by working extra hard, determined to succeed despite experiencing racism in schools

GENDER DIFFERENCES IN EDUCATIONAL ACHIEVEMENT

Until 1980s the underachievement of girls was the major concern. However since 1990s girls started to outperform boys in all areas of the education system.

At GCSE girls tend to do better in the majority of subjects:

- 63.4% of girls and 53.8% of boys achieved 5+ A*-C GCSEs or equivalent in 2006 – a gender gap of 9.6%
- largest gender differences (a female advantage of more than 10% on those gaining an A*-C GCSE) are for the Humanities, the Arts and Languages
- smaller gender differences (a female advantage of 5% or less) tend to be in Science and Maths subjects
- girls are more likely than boys to gain an A* grade at GCSE
- boys are a little more likely to gain a G grade at GCSE or to gain no GCSEs at all

At A –Level gender differences in pass rate are much narrower but gender differences still remain:

- across all subjects, the range of difference is 4%. This is in the context of a very high pass rate
- girls perform better than boys in terms of those attaining an A grade (for the majority of subjects), which is a significant change over the last ten years

NOTE: Gender is not the strongest predictor of attainment:

- social class attainment gap at Key Stage 4 (as measured by percentage point difference in attainment between those eligible and not eligible for free school meals) is three times as wide as the gender gap
- some minority ethnic groups attain significantly below the national average and their under-achievement is much greater than the gap between boys and girls

Why are girls doing better than boys?

Mitos and Browne (1998) found

1. the women's movement and feminism raised girls' expectations and self-esteem
2. the increasing number of employment opportunities for women
3. many girls' mother are in paid employment and act as positive role models for them
4. girls' priorities have changed: Sue Sharpe (1976) 'Just Like a Girl'
5. girls are better motivated and organised than boys
6. girls at 16 are seen to be more mature than boys
7. girls benefitted from introduction of coursework in GCSEs/A-Levels
8. national curriculum made more subjects compulsory
9. teachers less likely to gender stereotype girls into set roles or careers

Why do boys underachieve?

1. boys are generally more disruptive in class than girls
2. boys appear to gain 'street cred' by not working hard
3. decline in traditional male jobs
4. teachers tend to have lower expectations of boys

5. lack of male role models in schools
6. laddish subcultures
7. identity crisis in men – uncertain future removes purpose in achieving
8. boys do not like reading as it has become feminised
9. boys tend to overestimate their ability
10. feminisation of assessment – coursework rather than competitive exams

Teacher-pupil interaction affecting the gender gap?

1. Michael Barber (1996) found boys tend to over-estimate their ability, with GCSE results showing the opposite to be true
2. Michelle Stanworth (1983) found boys dominated classroom interaction, pushing girls to the margins which lowered their self-confidence and made them feel less valued, hence girls underestimating their ability
3. Dale Spender (1982) found teachers gave priority to boys giving the impression what girls said was less important
4. Howe (1997) identified the different ways teachers interact with boys and girls - such differences in interaction emerge very early, even in preschool.

Masculine identity can be seen as incompatible with academic success

1. **Forde** (2006) boys are more likely to be influenced by their male peer group which might devalue schoolwork and so put them at odds with academic achievement. It is argued that girls do not experience a conflict of loyalties between friends and school to the same extent as boys
2. **Jackson** 2002 found disruptive behaviour will have a number of benefits by increasing a boy's status with his peer group and can it can deflect attention away from academic performance
3. **Kelly** (1987) found science and the science classroom remain 'masculine' environments with boys dominating science classrooms

Are Changes in the Examination System Responsible for the Gender Gap?

1. Stobart (1992) found a direct relationship between the relative improvement of girls' achievement and the weighting and type of coursework required in different subjects
2. Perceptions of girls' perceived advantage in coursework is high amongst teachers. Over half (53%) of teachers felt that that there was a difference between boys' and girls' ability to do coursework Bishop (1996)

Effects of gender socialization

1. **Lobban** (1974) found evidence of gender stereotyping in children's books with women occupying traditional roles. Best (1993) found little had changed in almost 20 years

2. **Kelly** (1987) – gender stereotyping in science classrooms as well as science text books where women are largely invisible

Changes in society

1.   Beck (1992) argues in the risk society the rise of individualism allows women to become more self-reliant and self-sufficient through education

ETHNICITY AND ACHIEVEMENT IN SCHOOL

The achievement of ethnic minority pupils in British schools is very complex but the Swann Report of 1985 examined the underachievement of some ethnic minority groups. It is important not to see ethnic minorities as a homogenized (single) group. This is because the patterns of achievement are varied.

Pupils of Indian and Chinese origin tend to do very well, out-performing both the average and the scores of white pupils. By contrast, pupils of Pakistani origin show a very varied pattern of achievement with some doing very well and others relatively poorly. Nevertheless minority ethnic groups tend to underachieve when compared to other population groups.

Your revision will be made easier by using the same approach as used above. Remember to isolate **factors inside school** from those **factors outside school**. Similarly refer back to the previous sections on social-class backgrounds; speech and language codes as well as material and cultural factors.

First some facts (Runnymede Trust, June 2012) which highlight the wide variation across ethnic minority groups:

- Attainment – GCSES (5 A*-C grades including Maths and English) Attainment by ethnicity has improved since 2006/7, and achievement gaps between some ethnic groups and the national level have disappeared. Other ethnic groups, such as Chinese students, have far higher levels of attainment compared to the national level. It is worth highlighting however that Pakistani and Black Caribbean young people still have lower attainment levels than the national level. The data for 2010/11 is as follows:

1. The national level, and the percentage of White British pupils achieving 5 A*-C grades including Maths and English, is 58%. This compares to around 45% in 2006/07

2. Chinese students are the highest attaining group, with 78.5% achieving 5 A*-C grades including Maths and English. This compares to 70% in 2006/07

3. Indian students are the second highest attaining group, with 74.4% achieving 5 A*-C grades including Maths and English. This compares to around 62% in 2006/07

4. Bangladeshi pupils now have a slightly higher attainment rate than White pupils, with 59.7% 5 A*-C grades including Maths and English. This is a massive improvement given that only around 40% achieved this 2006/07, which was 5% less than White pupils and the National Level

5. There has also been an improvement for Black African pupils, with 57.9% achieving 5 A*-C grades including Maths and English, compared to just over 40% achieving this in 2006/07. A similar level of improvement can be seen for mixed White and Black African pupils

6. However, Pakistani and Black Caribbean young people still have lower attainment levels compared to the national level, with 52.6% and 48.6% respectively achieving 5 A*-C grades including Maths and English. This has, however, improved from around 35% for Pakistani and 34% for Black Caribbean pupils in 2006/07

7. Travellers, Gypsies and Roma are still the lowest achieving groups, with 17.5% of Irish Travellers and 10.8% of those from Gypsy or Roma backgrounds achieving 5 A*-C grades including Maths and English.

This has improved from 2006/07 when only 5% of these groups combined achieved the required grades.

Factors Outside School

- Social class and material factors – African-Caribbean and Bangladeshi Asians are more likely to be working-class and in poverty and so have a general material disadvantage while Indian and African Asian children are more likely to come from professional/business middle-class backgrounds and the subsequent advantages

- Language – In some ethnic minority households English is not the main language which might cause problems in doing some school work/communication with teachers – but the Swann Report (1985) found language factors were of little importance for the majority as did Modood (1997) who found the high attainment of Indian pupils suggested a second language was not a barrier to achievement

- Racism outside school – Stuart Hall identified a 'culture of resistance' among African-Caribbean youths as a reaction to racial prejudice in society

- Family life – some minority ethnic groups have stronger parental support than others. African-Caribbean have high levels of lone-parenthood and the subsequent material problems. Tony Sewell (1997) argued African-Caribbean boys growing up in lone parent households lacked male role models found in father figure. In contrast Asian family families tend to be extended families offering high levels of support. In addition Archer (2006) found Chinese students and parents put a high value on education as it gave the family a high standing in their community.

Factors Inside School

- Ethnocentric curriculum - school curriculum and the hidden curriculum is too focused on white British culture and adds to the low self-esteem and underachievement of ethnic minorities.

- Racism inside school - The Swann Report found only a small number of teachers were consciously racist. But - Wright (1992) found teachers treated ethnic minority children differently to White children and Gillborn (1990) found African-Caribbean students were more likely to be criticised compared to other ethnic groups committing the same offence – could this lead to Hargreaves self-fulfilling prophecy or Stuart Hall's culture of resistance? Browne (2008) argues negative labelling does not necessarily lead to the negative effects of the self-fulfilling prophecy – see Fuller page 24.

- Setting and streaming - evidence suggests that Black pupils are more likely to be entered for lower tier exams, meaning that these students are only able to able to achieve a maximum grade of a C grade. Stephen J. Ball (2008) has found that Black Caribbean and African students are less likely to be identified for gifted and talented programmes. In contrast, evidence also suggests that Chinese and Indian students are more likely to be entered into higher sets

- Exclusions and discipline - research by David Gillborn and David Drew (2010) found that excluded pupils are 4 times more likely to finish their education without having gained academic qualification. Research by the former Department for Education and Skills (Getting it, Getting it Right 2006) suggest a number of reasons as to why Black pupils are disproportionately excluded, including institutional racism. The same report also found Black pupils encounter both conscious and unconscious prejudice from teachers (both in terms of frequency and severity).

Note: Now you have finished this unit you might like to test your subject knowledge using our multiple choice test book which is also available to purchase at Amazon.

3 RESEARCH METHODS

Positivism and interpretivism are two distinct principles which shape the reasoning behind research methods:

Positivists use quantitative research methods. These methods produce quantitative data which is information presented in numerical form such as graphs and charts. In contrast sociologists adopting an interpretivist approach to social research prefer to use qualitative research methods. These methods generate qualitative data such as in-depth insights into respondents thoughts and feelings, along with the meanings they give to events rather than numerical data.

The core principles of positivism (quantitative methods) are:

- social scientific research is based on logic with a clear methodology
- research must be objective throughout all processes
- the role of theory is to generate a hypothesis (prediction) which can be tested
- look for cause and effect (patterns of behaviour) in order to uncover universal laws about the social world – what Durkheim termed social-facts
- positivists use quantitative methods

The core principles of interpretivism (qualitative methods) are:

- interpretivists are anti-positivist in principle as they are skeptical about sociology's scientific status
- they reject the view human behaviour is predictable in the same way the natural world is seen to be
- unlike molecules, human beings are conscious entities and act with purpose
- intrepretivists argue human behaviour is not the result of external forces (social facts) instead sociologists need to understand the meaning and motivations behind individual action by seeing the world through their eyes – this is known as verstehen
- interpretivists use qualitative methods

There are two types of quantitative and qualitative data - primary and secondary.

- primary data is that collected by sociologists themselves through social surveys such as structured interviews
- secondary data is data which already exists such as that found in newspapers, novels, literature, letters, diaries, police records, school results, government reports etc.

Positivists prefer to collect quantitative data through the following research methods which are seen to collect reliable data:

- closed/structured questionnaires
- structured interviews
- the experiment
- the comparative method
- official statistics
- social surveys

Interpretivist primary methods include:

- participant and non-participant observations
- open-ended questionnaires
- informal or unstructured interviews

Quantitative secondary sources: a main source of quantitative secondary data comes from official sources such as local and national government and their associated agencies such as the Office for National Statistics (ONS) who gather data on births; deaths; marriages etc. to produce official statistics.

Advantages of official statistics

- they're relatively easy and inexpensive to access
- they're readily available
- they're often the only source of data on a topic area
- as they're so comprehensive they're more likely to be representative
- they're more likely to cover a long time span (crime figures and education data) and so it's easier to see the influence of government policies 'before and after'

Disadvantages of official statistics

- as official data isn't collect by sociologists, problems are likely in the recording and accuracy of the data, for example the British Crime Survey exists to overcome the 'dark-figures' of unrecorded crime
- some of these 'dark figures' come from policemen having to interpret a situation as being criminal or not. This shows how official data might not be as objective as expected
- officials recording data are doing so for administrate reasons and so they're not using terms and classifications used by sociological researchers
- official figures are sometimes 'massaged' by the state to avoid embarrassing the government of the day for example hospital waiting times

Secondary qualitative data is data which already exists such as:

Interpretivist secondary methods include:

- diary entries
- Facebook entries;
- letters and other personal accounts
- newspapers,
- novels
- police records,

- government reports;
- school records;
- /parish registers
- content analysis

Advantages of secondary qualitative data:

- qualitative secondary sources are sometimes the only form of information available on a particular topic. For example Laslett's research on the family across several centuries wouldn't have been possible if records hadn't been kept. This shows how this form of documentation is useful for making comparisons over time
- qualitative secondary sources provide a gateway into the past allowing researchers to understand the concerns and attitudes of people at the time. This can be carried out by reading letter columns in newspapers as well as comment postings on online newspapers such as the Guardian for example
- analysing historical documents is useful in allowing interpretivists to gain insights into the beliefs, values and ideologies held by their authors

Disadvantages of qualitative secondary sources of data:

- how credible is the evidence. An individual diary entry could be full of exaggerations and biases, moreover any entry could merely reflect the interests and beliefs of the author. For example autobiographies and diaries of politicians might contain selected content in order to portray the author in a more positive light
- how representative is the evidence? It could be that other documents which would challenge an account of are ignored in order to keep the author in a positive light, how credible is the evidence? For example newspaper accounts of an incident might reflected the values of the newspaper creating the report

Considerations any sociologist must make when choosing an appropriate method:

- **validity** – to what extent do the research findings provide a true picture of what was studied?
- **reliability** – will the findings be the same if the study is repeated?
- **representativeness** – will the sampling method produce results which are representative of the wider population in order for generalization to be made?
- **ethical issues** – will the research processes be structured around moral standards of behaviour?
- **pilot study** – designing a suitable trial-run in order to achieve a decent response rate
- **practicalities** – is there the time and money to conduct the chosen method?
- **the subjects** – is the selected method appropriate for the chosen respondents?
- **theoretical considerations** – sociologists preferences determines the selected method

Experimental method:

1. Scientists researching the natural sciences (physics, chemistry, biology) conduct their research in laboratories. They start with a hypothesis and use the scientific process to test whether their hypothesis was true or false. In the laboratory all the variables are kept constant expect the independent variable (the one you are testing).
2. In laboratories scientists are able to control the variables (e.g. temperature, light etc.) so an experiment can be undertaken in order to test out a hypothesis (a prediction which can be tested).
3. All the data is converted into numerical form (hence why positivist sociologists seek to do the same

thing).

4. Overcoming the Hawthorne Effect – where the researchers presence affects the behavior of those being studied

There are three types of experiments sociologists can use:

1. Lab experiment
2. Field experiment
3. Natural experiment

The advantages of laboratory experiments are:

- makes isolating and manipulating variables easier so causes of events can be identified
- other scientists can easily repeat the same experiment
- they're high in reliability as other researchers can replicate the same experiment and achieve the same results
- comparisons can be made with similar experimental research
- scientists can test their hypothesis in controlled conditions

The disadvantages of using the experimental method in sociology are:

- it's difficult to identify and isolate a single cause of any social issue such as the cause of crime, as there could be multiple causes
- because of the above, it's impossible to isolate variables for testing on their own in order to see if they are the cause. For example, the causes of underachievement at school could be subcultural or economic or dietary etc.
- as sociologists want to study people in their normal environment any laboratory setting becomes an artificial situation – it's not real life – a point exacerbated by the fact people would know they're being experimented on and so The Hawthorne Effect would undermine the validity of any experiment being conducted
- there are numerous ethical problems for the sociologist, particularly as the experimental group could suffer negative effects from the experiment being conducted on them. Another ethical issue is people might not want to be experimented on in the first place

Field experiments

- Field experiments occur in real-life conditions such as a school, while at the same time trying to follow similar procedures to those found in any laboratory experiment.
- Some experimental methods have been used in sociology and these are known as field experiments. Field experiments are conducted in the real world situations, such as a school. They tend to be carried out by interpretivists who are interested in looking for meanings which underpin everyday interaction in the social world.

Rosenthal and Jacobson conducted a field experiment in a school in 1968. This involved testing the hypothesis teacher expectations hand important effects on pupils academic performance, in order to see if the self-fulfilling prophecy existed.

- the trouble is this form of 'real-world' experiment is fraught with ethical problems as it could have been the teachers expectations and those students labelled with low expectations could have been damaged by the label

- positivists argue field experiments suffer from issues of reliability as the sociologist cannot control all the likely variables

Natural experiments: are conducted in natural environments (a laboratory is an artificial environment). One example would be studies of twins (to test out whether a cause is due to nature or nurture). However though natural experiments are very rare in 2015 NASA astronaut Scott Kelly and his twin, former astronaut Mark Kelly were part of a natural experiment to test the effects of long space missions on humans.

The comparative method

- The comparative method is built on the same principles as the experimental method discussed above but uses the real-world as the laboratory.
- Instead of setting up an experiment the researcher collects data, usually official statistics about different social groups (e.g. working-class; middle-class and upper-class) and then compares one group with another to identify what is evident in one group but not another.

Social surveys

Social surveys are popular with positivist sociologists because they can collect primary data from a large number of people, typically in a standardized statistical form.

1. The sociologist takes a random selection of a sample, which is representative of the population being studied.
2. This sample might be sent a standardized questionnaire through the post or asked to take part in a structured interview.
3. The benefit of this method is a large amount of data is compiled in a short time frame.

Some important social survey terms:

- Survey population – is the whole group being studied
- Sampling frame – is a list of names of all those included in the survey population from which the sample is selected
- Representative sample – a small group drawn from the survey population
- Sampling method – the techniques used to select a representative sample
- Hypotheses – is a statement which makes a prediction which is tested to either be true or false by the research
- Operationalisation – is a way of measuring an abstract concepts such as social-class

Most social surveys are conducted via postal questionnaires because:

Advantages of postal questionnaires:

- Tend to be cheap
- Can use larger samples
- Have a quick turnaround period
- Can be closed questions which are user-friendly
- Easily quantified

Disadvantages of postal questionnaires:

- Can be costly in regard to stamp prices
- Need return envelops
- Respondent needs incentive to return questionnaire
- Low response rate
- May not be representative
- Cannot control who completed questionnaire

Before you can give out a survey you need a sample:

Sampling: provides the researcher with a representative sample. A **sampling method** is chosen in order to achieve the most representative sample possible.

The main sampling methods are:

- **Random sampling** – people selected at random
- **Stratified random sampling** – a random sample is chosen from a subdivided group of people e.g. a specific age range
- **Quota sampling** – researcher selects people by a certain criteria e.g. gender
- **Snowball sampling** – the researcher selects a respondent meeting their requirements, then asks them to recommend someone meeting the same criteria
- **Cluster or multistage sampling** – selecting your sample in various stages e.g. 1st – take a random sample of hospital patients; 2nd – select a random sample from within those patients for your study
- **Systematic sampling** – selecting from the sampling frame at regular intervals until the size of sample is reached

Pilot study - once the researcher has selected their research method and their sample method it is a good idea to conduct a pilot study. A pilot study is a practice run, so you iron-out any logistical problems or issues with the questions being asked.

Questionnaires

- Questionnaires (like the postal questionnaire discussed above) are a common method of discovering sociological truths. If you're using positivist methods you'll have to make a closed or structured or pre-coded questionnaire in order to gather quantitative data.
- On the other hand, as a sociologist, you might wish to adopt an interpretivist approach and use open-ended or unstructured questionnaires.

Closed or structured or pre-coded questionnaires (quantitative)

Advantages

1. relatively quick to complete by respondent
2. easier, quick, and less costly to analyze
3. data produced ought to be reliable, (easy to repeat) allowing other researchers to test the findings (replicating the method of the natural scientists)
4. they produce data which is relatively easy to categorize and present in statistical form such as graphs and charts

5. make it easy for comparisons to be between different groups. This is because respondents are all answering the same questions

Disadvantages

1. possible misinterpretation of questions
2. limited choice of answers puts artificial limits on how the respondent answers
3. if answered with researcher present respondent might 'lie', as they're too embarrassed to tell the truth
4. the responses set out are those of the sociologist and not necessarily those of the respondent (imposition problem)
5. too many options might confuse the respondent
6. no way of knowing if respondent understood the question/questions
7. response options can put ideas into the respondents mind

Open or unstructured questionnaires (qualitative)

Advantages

1. responses are in the respondents own words, rather than those of sociologist as with closed questionnaires, which improves validity
2. the imposition problem found in closed questionnaires is less of an issue as the respondent is using their own words and not those of the researcher, as with closed questionnaires
3. they provide more detailed and deeper answers, including more information such as feelings and attitudes
4. open-ended questions simply do not allow respondents to speed read or avoid reading the questions and so "fill in" the answer without thinking

Disadvantages

1. with such a broad range of answers it can be hard to classify and quantify the data into graphs and charts
2. with such a broad range of answers it can be difficult to compare results with similar research
3. response rate can be lower than with those that use closed-ended questions, as people have to fill them in and they might feel awkward regarding their spelling and or hand-writing
4. responses might be 'skip' to the point as the respondent is in a rush and so the answers given are too vague
5. hand-writing might be illegible through the respondent rushing

Interviews

Structured Interviews (quantitative)

Advantages

1. There is less of a problem with interviewer bias than unstructured (open interviews) as there's less involvement of the interviewer
2. As they usually have pre-planned (pre-coded) questions, it's relatively easy to put the data gathered into statistical forms such as graphs (positivist in nature)
3. As the questions are pre-coded the data gathered is often seen as more reliable as all respondents are answering the same questions, which makes it easier to replicate the process by other interviewers

4. They're generally seen as a more effective way of getting questionnaires completed, particularly postal questionnaires which have a high non-response rate, particularly as it overcomes the problems of illiteracy

Disadvantages

1. Their pre-coded structure means it puts limits on what respondents can say a) which means the interviewer can't probe the respondent beyond what the set questions, b) these limitations mean it's difficult for the interviewer to gain understanding (verstehen) of what the respondents means
2. Although the advantage is seen to be the lack of interviewer bias, there is still remains a possibility of interviewer bias caused by non-verbal cues such as frowning
3. In regard to postal questionnaires and questionnaires, interviews are more costly (interviewers have to be paid and the interview process is much slower) than either postal questionnaires or questionnaires

Unstructured Interviews (qualitative)

Advantages

1. Often a good deal of rapport develops between interviewer and interviewee allowing detailed and honest information to be obtained. This is very useful where the subject being researched might be particularly sensitive
2. It allows the respondent (interviewee) to speak for themselves, so the researcher can gain a better understanding (verstehen) of the topic being discussed
3. The interviewer can easily develop points raised by the respondent to gain an even deeper meaning by exploring the meanings and motivations behind a particular action or event

Disadvantages

1. The success of the interview often depends on the quality and skills of the interviewer
2. The interview itself can be very time consuming and playing back what's been recorded is also very time consuming which means fewer interviews take place meaning samples tend to be small
3. As the interviews are open, the lack of non-standardized questions make generalization and the production of statistics difficult
4. There's a good chance of interviewer bias: a) The interviewer could give non-verbal cues such as smiling which could influence an interviewee's response b) The interviewer may only follow up leads in the interview they deem important, which could contradict what the respondent feels as important
5. The fact you ask questions about something sometimes affects the dynamic of the interview to the extent the respondent changes their behaviour

Observations

When conducting participant observation the researcher can either observe covertly or overtly.

- Overt observation is where the researcher will disclose themselves to the participants so they know they're being observed.
- Covert observation is where those being observed are unaware they are being observed (the researcher's undercover – 'gone native'); this usually involves the researcher assuming a false identity for example, if you were researching the behaviour of football supporters you'd pretend you were a supporter so you could conduct the research.

A famous example was John Howard Griffin who dyed his skin black and lived as a black man in the southern states of America in 1960.

Advantages of participant observation

1. you have high validity doesn't disturb the normal behaviour of the group – no risk of the Hawthorne effect
2. no prior knowledge of social dynamic being observed is required
3. allows the observer to dig deeper into groups/individual behaviour
4. research can be sustained over a long period of time giving greater depth
5. seen as being high in validity -can see how people really behave
6. it can generate new ideas and insights not previously considered
7. observes first-hand in non-artificial surroundings
8. as they are over a sustained period, you can observe changes in behaviour over-time rather than as snapshot picture
9. only way to observe criminal gangs or other hostile groups
10. Hawthorne Effect

Disadvantages of participant observation

1. ethical issues just by participating in criminal activity
2. ethical issues if covertly witnessing criminal activity
3. tend to be small scale and the group being studied might not be typical
4. the researcher may be exposed to danger for example, if participating in criminal activity
5. if the identity of researcher is uncovered the whole research could be ruined
6. the participants may feel betrayed and used if/when they find out their activities were being recorded and could take out revenge
7. difficult to record observations without being found out
8. difficult to leave the group having been a part of the group for so long
9. difficult to remain covert for long periods of time

Positivists question the reliability of participant observation because they are difficult to replicate and so check the validity of any findings. Non- participant observation is conducted when the sociologists observes people in their normal setting without the presence of the researcher to avoid Hawthorne Effect for example observing a teacher via video camera.

Ethnographic studies

- Are sometimes better known as anthropological studies, where the researcher observes a culture by joining the group
- They are small-scale fieldwork producing qualitative data that are seen as valid as the research is conducted in natural settings
- It's hard to make any generalizations from these studies as they're small-scale

Secondary sources of data

Secondary sources of data can be quantitative and qualitative

Quantitative secondary sources: a main source of quantitative secondary data comes from official sources such as local and national government and their associated agencies such as the Office for National Statistics (ONS) who gather data on births; deaths; marriages etc. to produce official statistics (see page 33)

Content analysis

Content analysis involves the analysis of 'messages' in mass media content such as TV programmes, newspapers, magazines etc. (secondary sources) which can generate both quantitative and qualitative data.

Strengths

- Low cost
- Can make comparisons over time (longitudinal study)
- Quantitative analysis is seen as reliable

Weaknesses

- Time consuming
- Qualitative studies are highly subjective
- Assumes the media has had an effect on the audience
- Personal documents

Secondary qualitative data is data which already exists such as:

Diaries; letters; etc which provide a rich source of qualitative data on feeling; motives etc (see page 33)

Strengths

- Provide a rich insight into a person's feelings and motivations
- They are usual in providing insights where no other data exists such as being held captive
- They are often the only insight sociologists have into the past such as war veterans diaries or letters home
- Personal documents can supplement official data such as school performance. A school might be high in league tables but pupils dislike the regime in which they learn

Weakness

- They are a one person view of events which can be biased in order to justify a person's actions and therefore invalid
- The data is likely to be unreliable
- The data is likely to be unrepresentative

- The authenticity of the data is open to question
- The sociologist might interpret the data in a way the author never intended

Case Studies and life histories

- Case studies are where the sociologist undertakes an intensive study of the topic or case being studied usually using interpretivist methods such as open-interviews or participant observations.

- Life histories study one individual again through interpretivist methods such as unstructured interviews along with any personal documents to validate what is said.

Strengths of case studies and life histories

1. useful in generating new hypotheses
2. allows the researcher to see the world from another perspective

Weakness

1. may not be representative
2. any interpretation of past events is seen from a contemporary perspective

Historical and public documents

- These are reports made by governments; companies; trade unions; schools; hospital trusts etc; therefore they can be contemporary (current) or historical (from the past).

Strengths of public and historical documents are:

- They are more than likely the only way we can gain insights into past events
- They allow comparisons over time for example, birth; death and marriage rates
- They are useful when assessing the outcomes of various social policies such as raising the school leaving age

Weaknesses of public and historical documents

- The validity of the documents are open to question, as they may have been written selectively
- The documents content is open to misinterpretation
- The authenticity of a document is open to question as it might not have been written by the person it is attributed to; therefore undermining its reliability

Triangulation sometimes referred to as methodological pluralism

- Triangulation is the use of one or more research methods when carrying out social research in order for the different methods to complement each other.

- For example, Ofsted using overt observations as well as official data (exam results) to assess how well as school is performing. The trouble is triangulation produces a lot of data which takes a long time to process.

Longitudinal studies

Data is collected at regular intervals over a period of years.

Strengths

- provide detailed analysis of changes over time e.g. Seven-UP TV programme
- as with Seven-UP the sample remained the same, providing possible evidence of causes to any recorded changes
- as with Seven-UP recorded data is high in validity as not dependent on human memory for data which is liable to forgetfulness or exaggeration

Weaknesses

- as with Seven-UP sample size might dwindle due to people withdrawing or dying
- the Hawthorne Effect
- continuing such studies over time can be costly

Note: Now you have finished this unit you might like to test your subject knowledge using our multiple choice test book which is also available to purchase at Amazon.

4 GLOSSARY

Anthropology – studying the societies and cultures, especially those of pre-industrial societies found around the globe

Bourgeoisie – a term from Marxism denoting a social-class composed of people whose livelihood comes from the ownership of capital

Capitalism – an economy based on the production of goods for sale (commodities) using waged labour; capitalists own the means of production in order to make profit.

Culture – the beliefs, values and customs of a society or social group

Ethnicity – the members of a social group who share common characteristics such as religion, language or race

Ethnography – a research method based on the detailed observation of a culture or group

Experiment/laboratory experiment –a research procedure which attempts to test a hypothesis by manipulating aspects of reality to see whether the outcome suggested by the hypothesis occurs.

Ideology – a system of ideas and beliefs which may reflect the interests of a particular social group

Institutional racism – discrimination against a particular ethnic or racial groups which is built on the processes, procedures and policies of an institution whether or not the discrimination is intended

Marketization of education - where parents have the power and choice to make a decision and "shop around" as consumers of education to see which is the best school to send their child to

Net-migration - The rate of people moving into a country less the number of people moving out of the same country

Patriarchy – a social system of male dominance based on assumptions of male superiority

Power – the capacity of individuals, groups, or social-classes to achieve goals and protect interests

Proletariat – a term from Marxism denoting a social-class of people whose livelihood comes from selling their labour in exchange for wages (see bourgeoisie)

Racism – belief that biologically rooted characteristics determine social activities and abilities as well as the inherent superiority and inferiority of different races

Self-fulfilling prophecy – happens when people act in response to behaviour which has been predicted of them which subsequently makes the prediction come true

Social class – classifications of people with broadly similar occupations, resources or styles of living

Social policy - are public services that aid the well-being of citizens

Society – the total entity formed by individuals and groups and their social relations most commonly located within a nation state

Stereotyping – where generalized qualities or attributes of a social group often prejudice the representation of that group

State – a set of institutions and system of government which exercises control over a specific geographical area and the population of that area.

Underclass – a concept used to characterize those occupying the lowest positions in society

Vocational education - educational training that provides practical experience in a particular occupational field such as learning a trade

Welfare state – the social and political institutions by which the state assumes a responsibility for the health and social welfare of its citizens

5 INDEX

A

absolute poverty - 4
academies -18
achievement-
and ethnicity -29
and gender – 26
and class - 22
achieved status – 9, 19
anti-school subculture - 24
ascribed status – 9, 19
asset – 1
average income - 4

B

basket of goods - 4
boys underachievement – 26
Breadline Britain – 5, 6

C

capital - 1
case study – 43
comparative method - 37
compensatory education-18, 23
comprehensive schools – 17
consensual definition poverty -5
consumption property -1
content analysis - 42
counter-school subculture - 24
covert observations – 40
cultural capital - 22
cultural deprivation – 22
culture of resistance - 30

D

deprivation index – 5
dependency culture -14
disposable income - 3
distribution of wealth -2
division of labour - 9

E

Education Act 1944 - 17
Education Reform Act 1988 - 17
Education Acton Zones - 18
elaborated speech codes - 23
ethics - 35
ethnicity and education - 29

ethnicity and poverty – 8
ethnocentric curriculum - 30

F

fatalism - 23
feminism
and education – 21
and poverty – 9, 16
feminization poverty -16
field experiment – 36
free market
and education -17
and welfare -12
free schools – 18
free school meals - 22
functional prerequisite
and education - 19
functionalism and education-19
functionalism – 9, 16
functional prerequisite – 19
future time orientation - 23

G

gender and education – 26
gendered language - 21
grammar schools - 17

H

habitus - 22
halo effect -23
Hawthorne Effect – 36, 41, 44
hidden Curriculum - 20
hypothesis – 35, 36, 37

I

ideological state apparatus - 19
imposition problems - 39
independent schools – 18
ideological state apparatus -
individualism
and education – 28
immediate gratification - 23
income - 1
interactionism – 23, 24
interviewer bias - 40
interviews – 39
isolating variables - 36

L

labelling theory - 23

laboratory method - 35
language and education - 23, 30
life histories - 42
lone-parent families – 9, 30
longitudinal studies – 44
long shadow of work - 19

M

marketable wealth -1
marketization – 17, 44
Marxism
and poverty – 10, 15
and education – 19
means tested - 14
medium income -4
methodological pluralism - 43

N

nanny state - 14
New Right and welfare– 3, 7
New Right and education-17, 18
non-participant observation -
41

O

objectivity - 33
observations - 40
Office for Standards in
Education (Ofsted) – 18
official poverty line - 7
official statistics - 34
Operation Head Start - 23
operationalization – 5, 37
overt observations - 40

P

paid work -8
participant observation - 41
particularistic values -19
patriarchy – 44
pilot study - 38
positivism – 33, 37
positive discrimination - 23
postal questionnaires - 37
postmodernism – 3, 8
poverty line -7
productive property -1
progressive taxation - 12
primary data - 33

primary socialization -14`
private schools – 18
pupil subcultures - 24

Q
qualitative data - 33
quantitative data - 33
questionnaires – 37, 38
quota sampling - 38

R
racism - 30
random sampling - 38
redistribution wealth -
reliability – 34, 35
relative poverty - 5
representative sample - 38
research methods - 33
restricted speech codes – 23
Rowntree – 4, 7
role allocation – 19
ruling-class – 2, 7, 19

S
sample - 38
sample frame - 37
sample method - 38
secondary data - 42
secondary modern schools - 17
secondary data - 42
secondary socialization - 19
selection test - 17
self-fulfilling prophecy- 24, 35, 36
setting – 24, 30
social-class differences in educational achievement – 22
social construction – 5
social exclusion -
social facts - 32
social policies
and education – 17, 18
and welfare - 12
social research - 33
social surveys – 37
state provision -11
stratified random sample - 38
streaming – 24, 30
structured interviews – 39
structural differentiation - 4

sub-cultures – 14, 15, 24
Sutton Trust - 22

T
tax avoidance - 9
tax evasion –9
Third Sector - 11
Third Way – 12
Townsend -
triangulation - 43
tripartite system – 17

U
underachievement
and ethnicity - 29
and gender - 26
and social-class - 22
underclass – 3, 44
unearned income – 1
universal benefits - 14
universalistic values - 19
unstructured interview - 40

V
validity – 35
value consensus – 19
variables – 35, 36
verstehen – 33, 40
vocational education – 17, 18

W
wealth – 1
Weber – 9, 16
welfare – 11
welfare benefits
welfare dependency – 14
welfare pluralism - 11
welfare policies – 12, 13

6 FOR YOUR NOTES

ABOUT THE AUTHOR

The contents of the book have been written by sociologytwynham.com. For any other information or question you would like answering please contact us via the website. For other information on books in the series please visit the Revision page at sociologytwynham.com.